SHE
S

DIY Meals, Buckets, and Kits That Last 25 Years

By Jill Brady

SHELF-STABLE SURVIVAL

Disclaimer and/or Legal Notices:

While every attempt has been made to verify the information provided in this publication, neither the Author nor the Publisher assumes any responsibility for errors, omissions, or contrary interpretation of the subject matter herein. This publication is not intended for use as a source of legal or accounting advice. The Publisher wants to stress that the information contained herein may be subject to varying state and/or local laws or regulations. All users are advised to retain competent counsel to determine what state and/or local laws or regulations may apply to the user's particular business.

The Purchaser or Reader of this publication assumes responsibility for the use of these materials and information. Adherence to all applicable laws and regulations, federal, state, and local, governing professional licensing, business practices, advertising, and all other aspects of doing business in the United States or any other jurisdiction is the sole responsibility of the Purchaser or Reader. The Author and Publisher assume no responsibility or liability whatsoever on the behalf of any Purchaser or Reader of these materials. Any perceived slights of specific people or organizations are unintentional.

TABLE OF CONTENTS

INTRODUCTION

There's something deeply reassuring about a well-stocked pantry. When you open the door and see rows of neatly labeled jars, sealed buckets, and organized supplies, you're not just looking at food—you're looking at security, independence, and peace of mind. In uncertain times, knowing that you and your family can eat well for months or even years without relying on grocery stores or supply chains is more than practical. It's empowering.

This book is your guide to creating a complete, long-term food storage system using simple ingredients, affordable tools, and time-tested preservation methods. You don't need expensive commercial survival kits or specialized equipment to build a 25-year food supply. What you need is knowledge, a little time, and the willingness to take control of your family's food security.

Throughout these pages, you'll learn how to transform everyday staples into shelf-stable meals that last decades. You'll discover how to preserve proteins, package grains, dehydrate vegetables, and assemble complete meal kits that require nothing more than water and heat. You'll understand the science behind food preservation—what makes food spoil and how to prevent it. Most importantly, you'll gain the confidence to build a food storage system tailored to your family's needs and budget.

This isn't about fear or doomsday scenarios. It's about self-reliance, preparedness, and the satisfaction of knowing you've taken practical steps to protect what matters most. Our ancestors understood the importance of putting food by for lean times. They dried meat, stored grains, and preserved harvests not out of paranoia, but out of wisdom. We're simply applying those same principles with modern tools and knowledge.

Whether you're preparing for natural disasters, economic uncertainty, or simply want the peace of mind that comes from a well-stocked pantry, this book will show you how. Let's begin building your shelf-stable survival system—one jar, one bucket, one meal at a time.

CHAPTER 1: FOUNDATIONS OF SHELF-STABLE LIVING

Understanding shelf stability is the cornerstone of successful long-term food storage. When we talk about foods that last 25 years or more, we're not discussing magic or luck—we're talking about science, proper technique, and creating an environment where bacteria, mold, and chemical breakdown simply cannot occur.

WHAT MAKES FOOD SHELF-STABLE?

Food spoilage happens through three primary mechanisms: **microbial growth** (bacteria, mold, and yeast), **enzymatic activity** (natural chemical processes within the food), and **oxidation** (reaction with oxygen that causes rancidity and nutrient loss). To create truly shelf-stable food, we must eliminate or control all three of these factors.

Microorganisms need four things to survive and multiply: **moisture**, **oxygen**, **favorable temperature**, and **time**. By removing moisture through dehydration, eliminating oxygen with absorbers and sealed packaging, and storing food in cool, dark conditions, we create an environment where nothing can grow or spoil. This is the fundamental principle behind every preservation method in this book.

THE FOUR ENEMIES OF FOOD STORAGE

Moisture is perhaps the most critical factor. Water activity in food provides the medium for bacterial growth and chemical reactions. When we reduce moisture content below 10%, most microorganisms cannot survive. This is why properly dried foods can last indefinitely when sealed away from humidity.

Oxygen causes fats to go rancid, vitamins to degrade, and creates conditions for aerobic bacteria to thrive. By using oxygen absorbers and vacuum-sealing, we create an anaerobic environment that preserves food quality and prevents spoilage.

Light breaks down vitamins, changes colors, and accelerates chemical deterioration. This is why we store food in opaque containers or dark locations. Even foods sealed in Mylar bags benefit from being kept in buckets or closets away from light exposure.

Temperature affects the rate of all chemical reactions. For every 10-degree increase in storage temperature, food deterioration roughly doubles in speed. This is why cool, stable temperatures—ideally between 50-70°F—are essential for maximum shelf life.

ESSENTIAL STORAGE MATERIALS

Building your shelf-stable system requires just a few key materials, most of which are surprisingly affordable and readily available.

Mylar bags are your primary barrier against moisture, oxygen, and light. These metallized plastic bags come in various sizes, from one-quart pouches perfect for spices to five-gallon liners for food buckets. Look for bags that are at least 5 mils thick for puncture resistance and long-term durability.

Oxygen absorbers are small packets containing iron powder that chemically binds with oxygen, reducing oxygen levels in sealed containers to nearly zero. They're rated by capacity—typically 100cc, 300cc, 500cc, or 2000cc. The size you need depends on the container volume and the food type. As a general rule, use 300cc absorbers for gallon-sized bags and 2000cc for five-gallon buckets.

Food-grade buckets provide rigid protection for Mylar bags and make storage and stacking easier. Five-gallon buckets with gamma seal lids are ideal because they're reusable, stackable, and easy to open without tools. Make sure any bucket you use is marked as food-grade—look for the recycling symbol with a "2" (HDPE) or "5" (PP) inside.

Mason jars are perfect for smaller quantities, especially for foods you'll access frequently. While glass jars with metal lids don't provide the same oxygen barrier as Mylar, they work beautifully for vacuum-sealed dry goods and are excellent for short-to-medium-term storage.

Vacuum sealers and heat sealers are your sealing tools. A simple impulse heat sealer (around $20-40) works perfectly for Mylar bags. For jars, a vacuum sealer with jar attachments removes air before sealing. Neither tool is complicated, and both pay for themselves quickly.

FOOD SAFETY FUNDAMENTALS

Safety must be your first priority when building a food storage system. Fortunately, the same techniques that create shelf stability also create safety.

Always start with **clean, dry containers and work surfaces**. Wash your hands thoroughly, and use clean utensils and scoops. While you're creating an environment where bacteria can't grow, you don't want to seal in contamination from the start.

Inspect all ingredients before packaging. Discard anything that shows signs of moisture, mold, insect damage, or off odors. Only package foods that are completely dry and in good condition.

Label everything with the contents, packaging date, and any relevant information like source or variety. Use permanent markers or printed labels that won't fade. In five or ten years, you'll be grateful for clear labeling.

Monitor your storage area regularly. Check for signs of pest activity, temperature fluctuations, or moisture. A simple thermometer and humidity gauge (available for under $10) helps you track conditions. Ideal storage maintains 50-70°F and below 15% humidity.

Rotate and inspect your stock periodically. While properly stored foods last decades, regular checks ensure your system is working. Look for any bags that have lost their vacuum seal, buckets with damaged lids, or jars showing condensation.

CREATING YOUR STORAGE SPACE

You don't need a massive basement or dedicated bunker to build an effective food storage system. A closet, under-bed space, garage shelving, or even a corner of a bedroom can work beautifully with proper organization.

Choose the **coolest, darkest, and driest** location available. Avoid areas near water heaters, furnaces, or exterior walls that experience temperature swings. Basements are ideal if they're dry; avoid damp basements or areas prone to flooding.

Elevate your storage off the floor using pallets, shelving, or plastic platforms. This protects against moisture, makes cleaning easier, and improves air circulation. Stackable buckets work well, but don't stack more than 4-5 high to avoid crushing bottom containers.

Organize by category and rotation date. Group similar items together—grains with grains, proteins with proteins. Place older items toward the front for first use. Consider creating a simple inventory sheet to track what you have and when it was packaged.

With these foundations in place, you're ready to start building your shelf-stable food system. In the next chapter, we'll design a balanced long-term food plan and begin creating your first complete meals.

CHAPTER 2: BUILDING THE DIY SURVIVAL SYSTEM

Creating a 25-year food supply isn't about randomly filling buckets with rice and beans. It's about designing a balanced, nutritious, and satisfying system that provides everything your body needs while remaining practical to store, affordable to build, and actually enjoyable to eat.

DESIGNING YOUR FOOD PLAN

A well-designed food storage system balances four essential elements: **proteins** for tissue repair and immune function, **carbohydrates** for energy, **fats** for hormone production and nutrient absorption, and **micronutrients** for overall health. Additionally, you need **flavor and variety** to maintain morale and prevent food fatigue.

The traditional "rice and beans" approach isn't wrong—it's just incomplete. While rice and beans together provide complete protein and substantial calories, a diet of nothing but rice and beans quickly becomes monotonous and lacks essential vitamins and fats. Your goal is to create a diverse system that provides balanced nutrition and enough variety to sustain you comfortably.

CALCULATING YOUR NEEDS

Start by determining how many calories per day your household needs. The average adult requires 2,000-2,500 calories daily, with higher needs for physically active individuals, growing children, or cold climates. For planning purposes, calculate 2,200 calories per adult per day as a baseline.

For a one-year supply for one person, you'll need approximately 800,000 calories total. This breaks down into roughly:

- **400 pounds of grains** (wheat, rice, oats, pasta)
- **60 pounds of legumes** (beans, lentils, split peas)
- **16 pounds of fats and oils**
- **60 pounds of sugar and sweeteners**
- **8 pounds of salt and seasonings**
- **20 pounds of powdered milk or protein**
- **Additional dehydrated vegetables, fruits, and flavor enhancers**

These numbers are guidelines, not rigid requirements. Adjust based on your family's preferences, dietary restrictions, and budget. The key is maintaining balance across all nutritional categories.

BUILDING BALANCED MEAL KITS

The most practical approach to long-term storage is creating **complete meal kits**—pre-measured combinations of ingredients that make full meals with minimal preparation. This approach offers several advantages: it ensures balanced nutrition, simplifies meal planning during emergencies, and makes rotation and use much easier.

BASIC SOUP MIX

This versatile base creates hearty, nutritious soups with just water and heat.

Ingredients:

- 1 cup dried lentils
- 1 cup split peas (green or yellow)
- ½ cup dried carrots (diced small)
- ½ cup dried celery
- ¼ cup dried onion flakes
- 2 tablespoons chicken or vegetable bouillon powder
- 1 teaspoon dried thyme
- 1 teaspoon dried parsley
- ½ teaspoon black pepper
- ½ teaspoon garlic powder

Instructions:

1. Divide into portions (about 2 cups per meal serving 4 people)
2. Package each portion in a quart-sized Mylar bag with a 300cc oxygen absorber
3. Seal and label with contents and cooking instructions
4. Store in a cool, dark location

To Cook: Add one package to 8 cups of water, bring to a boil, then simmer 45-60 minutes until peas and lentils are tender. Add salt to taste.

Notes: This mix stores for 20+ years when properly sealed. You can add dried meat powder or jerky pieces when cooking for additional protein and flavor.

COMPLETE RICE & BEANS MEAL

A classic combination that provides complete protein and substantial calories.

Ingredients:

- 1 cup dried pinto or black beans
- 1 cup white rice (long-grain or parboiled)
- ¼ cup dried bell peppers
- 2 tablespoons dried onion flakes
- 1 tablespoon chili powder
- 2 teaspoons cumin
- 1 teaspoon garlic powder
- 1 teaspoon salt
- ½ teaspoon black pepper

Instructions:

1. Place beans in a small zip bag and the remaining dry ingredients (rice, vegetables, and seasonings) in a separate bag. Store both inside a one-gallon Mylar bag with a 500cc oxygen absorber.
2. Label the Mylar bag with cooking directions and seal for long-term storage in a cool, dark place.

To Cook: Remove the bean pouch and soak overnight or quick-soak by boiling 2 minutes and letting sit 1 hour. Drain, then cook beans in 4 cups water until tender, about 1 hour. Add the rice mix with 2 more cups water and simmer 20 minutes until rice is cooked and mixture thickens. Season to taste.

Notes: This makes approximately 8 servings. For faster cooking during emergencies, consider using split peas or lentils instead of beans—they cook in 30-45 minutes without soaking.

SCALING TO BUCKETS

Once you've tested and perfected your meal kit recipes in small batches, scaling up to five-gallon buckets becomes straightforward. A five-gallon bucket holds approximately 35-40 pounds of dry goods, depending on density.

Bucket Layering Method:

1. Line your clean, dry bucket with a 5-mil Mylar bag, leaving several inches of bag extending above the bucket rim
2. Add your food in layers, gently shaking to settle contents and eliminate air pockets
3. Leave 2-3 inches of headspace at the top
4. Add appropriate oxygen absorbers (typically 2000cc for a full bucket)
5. Seal the Mylar bag with a heat sealer, working from one end to the other to push out excess air
6. Fold the remaining Mylar down into the bucket and snap on the lid
7. Label the bucket exterior with contents, date, and weight

Bucket Meal Kit Example: Family Breakfast Bucket

This bucket provides approximately 30 breakfast servings for a family of four.

Contents:

- 10 pounds rolled oats (quick or old-fashioned)
- 5 pounds powdered milk
- 3 pounds dried fruit mix (apples, raisins, cranberries)
- 2 pounds brown sugar
- 1 pound chopped nuts (if fresh and properly stored)
- 8 ounces cinnamon
- 4 ounces salt

Instructions:

1. Place all bags in a five-gallon bucket
2. Add a 2000cc oxygen absorber to the bucket for extra protection
3. Seal bucket and label clearly

To Use: Open one ingredient bag at a time as needed. Combine ½ cup oats, 2 tablespoons powdered milk, 2 tablespoons dried fruit, 1 tablespoon sugar, and spices per serving. Cook with water according to oatmeal package directions.

STORAGE COMPARISON TABLE

Understanding which storage method works best for different foods helps you make informed decisions. Here's a quick reference guide:

Food Category	Best Container	Oxygen Absorber	Expected Shelf Life	Notes
White Rice	Mylar + Bucket	2000cc (5-gal)	25–30 years	Avoid brown rice — oils shorten shelf life
Dried Beans	Mylar + Bucket	2000cc (5-gal)	25–30 years	May require longer cooking as they age
Pasta	Mylar + Bucket	2000cc (5-gal)	30+ years	Excellent long-term staple
White Flour	Mylar + Bucket	2000cc (5-gal)	10–15 years	Rotate more often than whole grains
Oats (Rolled)	Mylar + Bucket	2000cc (5-gal)	25–30 years	Quick oats work well too
Dried Vegetables	Mylar Bags	300cc (1-gal)	15–25 years	Ensure contents are completely dry
Meat Powder	Mylar Bags	500cc	20–25 years	Remove all fat before storage
Jerky	Mylar Bags	300cc	5–10 years	Shorter life due to fat content
Powdered Milk	Mylar + Bucket	2000cc (5-gal)	10–20 years	Non-fat varieties last longest
Sugar	Sealed Container	Not needed	Indefinite	Moisture is the main enemy
Salt	Sealed Container	Not needed	Indefinite	Stores indefinitely if kept dry
Honey	Original Container	Not needed	Indefinite	May crystallize but remains safe
Spices (Ground)	Mylar or Jars	100cc	5–10 years	Gradual loss of flavor over time
Cooking Oil	Dark Bottles	Not effective	1–2 years	Rotate frequently to maintain freshness
Coconut Oil	Original Container	Not needed	2–3 years	Naturally solid at room temperature

TERIYAKI JERKY

A sweet and savory variation that adds variety to your protein storage.

Ingredients:

- 2 pounds lean beef, venison, or turkey (sliced ¼ inch thick against the grain)
- ¾ cup soy sauce
- ¼ cup Worcestershire sauce
- ¼ cup brown sugar
- 2 tablespoons honey
- 2 tablespoons rice vinegar
- 1 tablespoon fresh ginger (minced) or 1 teaspoon ground ginger
- 2 teaspoons garlic powder
- 1 teaspoon onion powder
- ½ teaspoon black pepper
- ¼ teaspoon red pepper flakes (optional)

Instructions:

1. Combine all marinade ingredients in a bowl, stirring until sugar dissolves
2. Add meat strips and marinate 8-24 hours in refrigerator
3. Remove meat and pat dry with paper towels
4. Arrange on dehydrator trays without overlapping
5. Dehydrate at 160°F for 5-7 hours until dry but still pliable
6. Cool completely before packaging
7. Package in Mylar bags with 300cc oxygen absorbers
8. Seal and label with date

Notes: This sweeter jerky may have slightly shorter shelf life due to sugar content. Plan to use within 3-5 years for best quality.

SPICY CAJUN JERKY

For those who enjoy heat and bold flavors.

Ingredients:

- 2 pounds lean beef, venison, or turkey (sliced ¼ inch thick against the grain)
- ½ cup soy sauce
- ¼ cup Worcestershire sauce
- 2 tablespoons hot sauce
- 2 tablespoons Cajun seasoning
- 1 tablespoon paprika
- 1 tablespoon garlic powder
- 1 tablespoon onion powder
- 1 tablespoon black pepper
- 1 teaspoon cayenne pepper (adjust to taste)
- 1 teaspoon dried thyme

Instructions:

1. Combine all ingredients in a bowl, mix well.
2. Add meat strips and marinate 12–24 hours in the refrigerator.
3. Drain, pat dry, and arrange on dehydrator trays.
4. Dehydrate at 160°F for 5–7 hours until dry but pliable.
5. Cool, package in Mylar with oxygen absorbers, and label.

CHICKEN POWDER

An alternative to beef that provides variety in your protein storage.

Ingredients:

- 2 pounds cooked ground chicken (fully cooked, drained, and cooled)
- 1 tablespoon salt (optional)

Instructions:

1. Drain all fat and juices completely
2. Rinse under hot water to remove additional fat
3. Spread on dehydrator trays in thin layer
4. Dehydrate at 145-160°F for 8-12 hours until completely dry and brittle
5. Cool completely
6. Grind in food processor to fine powder
7. Package immediately in Mylar bags with oxygen absorbers
8. Seal and label

To Use: Rehydrate with equal parts powder and hot water. Use in soups, casseroles, or any recipe calling for ground chicken.

Notes: Chicken powder is milder than beef and works beautifully in cream-based soups and Asian-inspired dishes.

COMPLETE CHICKEN NOODLE SOUP MIX

A comforting classic that stores for years.

Ingredients:

- 1 cup dried egg noodles or pasta pieces
- 1 cup chicken powder
- 1 cup dried mixed vegetables (carrots, celery, peas)
- ¼ cup dried onion flakes
- 3 tablespoons chicken bouillon powder
- 1 tablespoon dried parsley
- 1 teaspoon garlic powder

- 1 teaspoon dried thyme
- ½ teaspoon black pepper
- ½ teaspoon celery seed

Instructions:

1. Package in gallon Mylar bags (about 2 cups per serving for 4-6 people)
2. Add 500cc oxygen absorber
3. Seal and label

To Cook: Add one package to 8 cups boiling water. Reduce heat and simmer 15-20 minutes until noodles are tender. Season with salt to taste.

HEARTY BEEF STEW MIX

A filling, nutritious meal that requires only water.

Ingredients:

- 1 cup freeze-dried beef chunks or beef powder
- 1 cup dried potato dice
- ½ cup dried carrots
- ½ cup dried celery
- ½ cup dried onion flakes
- ¼ cup dried peas
- ¼ cup dried corn
- 3 tablespoons beef bouillon powder
- 2 tablespoons tomato powder (or ¼ cup dried tomato flakes)
- 1 tablespoon garlic powder
- 1 teaspoon dried thyme
- 1 teaspoon dried rosemary
- 1 teaspoon black pepper
- ½ teaspoon paprika

Instructions:

1. Package in gallon Mylar bags
2. Add 500cc oxygen absorber
3. Seal and label

To Cook: Add package to 8 cups boiling water. Reduce heat and simmer 30-40 minutes until vegetables are tender. Stir occasionally and add water if needed.

INSTANT REFRIED BEANS MIX

Quick, easy, and delicious side dish or burrito filling.

Ingredients:

- 4 cups cooked pinto or black beans (fully mashed before dehydration)
- ¼ cup dried onion flakes
- 2 tablespoons chili powder
- 1 tablespoon cumin
- 1 tablespoon garlic powder
- 2 teaspoons salt
- 1 teaspoon black pepper
- ½ teaspoon cayenne pepper (optional)

Preparation of Dehydrated Refried Beans:

1. Drain and mash beans thoroughly (or use potato masher)
2. Spread mashed beans thinly on dehydrator trays lined with non-stick sheets
3. Dehydrate at 135°F for 8-12 hours until completely dry and brittle
4. Break into pieces and grind to powder in food processor

Assembly:

1. Package in quart Mylar bags (about 1 cup per serving for 4 people)
2. Add 300cc oxygen absorber
3. Seal and label

To Use: Mix 1 cup bean powder with 1½ cups hot water. Stir well and let stand 10 minutes. Add more water if needed for desired consistency.

CORNBREAD MIX

Perfect companion to soups and stews.

Ingredients:

- 2 cups cornmeal
- 2 cups white flour
- 1 cup powdered milk
- ½ cup sugar
- 2 tablespoons baking powder
- 2 tablespoons salt

Instructions:

1. Package in quart Mylar bags (about 2 cups per batch)
2. Add 300cc oxygen absorber
3. Seal and label

To Make Cornbread: Combine 2 cups mix with 1 cup water and 2 tablespoons oil (if available). Mix until just combined. Pour into greased 8x8 pan and bake at 400°F for 20-25 minutes.

Notes: For off-grid baking, this can be cooked in a Dutch oven over coals or in a solar oven.

MASTER BAKING MIX

Versatile base for biscuits, pancakes, dumplings, and more.

Ingredients:

- 10 cups all-purpose flour
- ½ cup baking powder
- ¼ cup sugar
- 3 tablespoons salt
- 2 cups powdered milk
- 2 cups shortening

Instructions:

1. Cut in shortening until mixture resembles coarse crumbs
2. Package in gallon Mylar bags (about 3 cups per bag)
3. Add 500cc oxygen absorber
4. Seal and label

For Biscuits: Mix 2 cups mix with ½ cup water. Knead briefly, pat to ½-inch thickness, cut into rounds. Bake at 450°F for 10-12 minutes.

For Pancakes: Mix 2 cups mix with 1 cup water. Cook on griddle until bubbles form, flip and cook until golden.

For Dumplings: Drop spoonfuls of 2 cups mix + ¾ cup water into simmering soup. Cover and cook 15 minutes.

INSTANT PUDDING MIX

A morale-boosting dessert that stores well.

Ingredients:

- 1 cup sugar
- ½ cup cornstarch
- ¼ cup unsweetened cocoa powder (for chocolate) or vanilla powder (for vanilla)
- ½ teaspoon salt

Instructions:

1. Package in pint Mylar bags
2. Add 100cc oxygen absorber
3. Seal and label

To Make Pudding: Whisk one package with 2 cups cold water. Heat over medium heat, stirring constantly, until thickened. Cool and serve.

GRANOLA MIX

Nutritious breakfast or snack that provides energy and variety.

Ingredients:

- 4 cups rolled oats
- 2 cups chopped nuts (almonds, pecans, or walnuts)
- 1 cup unsweetened coconut flakes
- 1 cup dried fruit (raisins, cranberries, or chopped apples)
- ½ cup brown sugar
- ½ cup honey powder (or additional sugar)
- ¼ cup cinnamon
- 1 teaspoon salt

Instructions:

1. Combine sugar, cinnamon, and salt
2. Layer dry ingredients and sugar mixture in gallon Mylar bags
3. Add 500cc oxygen absorber
4. Seal and label

To Use: Eat dry as snack, or add milk and enjoy as cereal. Can also be mixed into oatmeal for extra nutrition and crunch.

Notes: Nuts reduce shelf life to 3-5 years due to oil content. For maximum longevity, package nuts separately and combine when ready to use.

TRAIL MIX ENERGY BLEND

High-calorie, nutrient-dense snack for emergencies or everyday use.

Ingredients:

- 1 cup dried fruit (raisins, cranberries, or banana chips)
- 2 cups nuts (almonds, cashews, peanuts)
- 1 cup chocolate chips or carob chips
- 1 cup sunflower seeds

- ½ cup pumpkin seeds
- ½ cup coconut flakes

Instructions:

1. Package in quart Mylar bags
2. Add 300cc oxygen absorber
3. Seal and label

Notes: Best consumed within 2-3 years due to nut and seed oils. Provides quick energy and essential fats.

CREAM OF WHEAT ALTERNATIVE

Hot breakfast cereal that cooks quickly and stores well.

Ingredients:

- 4 cups finely ground wheat, farina, or semolina
- 1 cup powdered milk
- ½ cup sugar
- ¼ cup cinnamon
- 1 teaspoon salt

Instructions:

1. Package in quart Mylar bags (about 1 cup per serving for 4 people)
2. Add 300cc oxygen absorber
3. Seal and label

To Cook: Bring 4 cups water to boil. Slowly whisk in 1 cup mix. Reduce heat and simmer 2-3 minutes, stirring constantly. Serve with dried fruit or honey.

A well-organized storage system saves time, reduces waste, and gives you confidence in your preparedness. Create a simple inventory system that tracks what you have, where it's stored, and when it was packaged.

Labeling Best Practices:

- Include: contents, quantity, packaging date, and location
- Add cooking instructions or serving sizes for meal kits
- Consider color-coding by category (proteins, grains, meals, etc.)

Rotation Strategy:

With your foundation built and your meal planning system in place, you're ready to dive into specific food categories. In the next chapter, we'll explore proteins—the most challenging and valuable component of long-term food storage.

CHAPTER 3: PROTEINS THAT LAST DECADES

Protein is the most challenging category in long-term food storage. Unlike grains and legumes, which store easily for decades, animal proteins contain fats that can go rancid and moisture that promotes bacterial growth. However, with proper preparation and storage techniques, you can preserve proteins that remain safe, nutritious, and delicious for 25 years or more.

HOMEMADE BEEF JERKY

Jerky is one of humanity's oldest preservation methods, and for good reason—it works beautifully. By removing moisture and adding salt, you create a protein-rich food that stores for years without refrigeration.

Basic Beef Jerky

Ingredients:

- 2 pounds lean beef (top round, flank, or sirloin), sliced ¼-inch thick
- ½ cup soy sauce
- ½ cup Worcestershire sauce

- 2 tablespoons brown sugar
- 2 tablespoons black pepper
- 1 tablespoon garlic powder
- 1 tablespoon onion powder
- 1 teaspoon liquid smoke (optional)
- 1 teaspoon red pepper flakes (optional)

Instructions:

1. Slice meat into ¼-inch thick strips, cutting against the grain for tender jerky or with the grain for chewier texture
2. Combine all marinade ingredients in a large bowl or zip-top bag
3. Add meat strips, ensuring all pieces are coated
4. Refrigerate 6-24 hours, turning occasionally
5. Arrange strips on dehydrator trays without overlapping
6. Dehydrate at 160°F for 4-6 hours until jerky bends without breaking and shows no moisture when bent
7. Allow to cool completely
8. Package in Mylar bags with oxygen absorbers
9. Seal and store in a cool, dark location

Notes: Properly dried and sealed jerky stores for 1-2 years at room temperature, or 5+ years in sealed Mylar with oxygen absorbers. For maximum shelf life, ensure jerky is completely dry—any remaining moisture reduces storage life.

MEAT POWDER: THE ULTIMATE PROTEIN STORAGE

Meat powder is a revelation for long-term storage. By grinding dried meat into powder, you create an incredibly versatile protein source that stores for decades, takes up minimal space, and rehydrates quickly in soups, stews, and sauces.

DIY Meat Powder

Ingredients:

- 2 pounds cooked lean beef, chicken, or venison (fully cooked and drained)
- 1 tablespoon salt (optional, for flavor)

Instructions:

1. Drain off all fat completely—this is critical for shelf life
2. Rinse the cooked meat under hot water to remove additional fat
3. Spread meat on dehydrator trays in a thin, even layer
4. Dehydrate at 145-160°F for 6-10 hours until completely dry and brittle
5. Allow to cool completely

6. Grind dried meat in a food processor or blender until it reaches a fine powder consistency
7. Package immediately in Mylar bags with oxygen absorbers
8. Seal and label with contents and date

To Rehydrate: Use 1 cup meat powder to 1 cup hot water. Let stand 10-15 minutes, then use in any recipe calling for ground meat.

Notes: One pound of fresh meat yields approximately 4 ounces of meat powder. Properly sealed meat powder stores for 20+ years and provides approximately 80% protein by weight.

MEAT POWDER SOUP MIX

This complete meal combines meat powder with vegetables and grains for a satisfying, protein-rich soup.

Ingredients:

- ½ cup meat powder (beef, chicken, or venison)
- 1 cup dried mixed vegetables
- ½ cup dried potato flakes
- ¼ cup dried onion flakes
- 3 tablespoons beef bouillon powder
- 1 teaspoon garlic powder
- 1 teaspoon dried thyme
- ½ teaspoon black pepper

Instructions:

1. Package in quart-sized Mylar bags (about 2 cups per bag)
2. Add 300cc oxygen absorber to each bag
3. Seal and label

To Cook: Add one package to 6 cups boiling water, reduce heat and simmer 15-20 minutes. Season with salt to taste.

CANNED MEAT STORAGE

While home-canned meat requires a pressure canner and careful technique, commercially canned meats offer an excellent alternative for long-term protein storage. Canned chicken, turkey, ham, salmon, and tuna store for 5-10 years in their original containers and require no special preparation.

Best Practices for Canned Meat:

- Store cans in cool, dark locations

- Rotate stock every 3-5 years for best quality
- Inspect cans regularly for rust, dents, or swelling
- Never use cans that are bulging, leaking, or severely dented

DRIED BEANS AND LEGUMES AS PROTEIN

While technically not animal protein, dried beans, lentils, and split peas deserve mention here because they're protein powerhouses that store beautifully. When combined with grains, they provide complete protein with all essential amino acids.

Long-Term Bean Storage:

1. Purchase dried beans in bulk (avoid canned beans for long-term storage)
2. Inspect for debris, damaged beans, or insect activity
3. Package in Mylar bags with oxygen absorbers
4. Seal and store in buckets or dark location
5. Label with variety and date

Best Varieties for Storage:

- Black beans
- Navy beans
- Kidney beans
- Lentils (red, green, or brown)
- Split peas (green or yellow)
- Chickpeas (garbanzo beans)

Properly stored dried beans last 25-30 years, though they may require longer cooking times as they age. Adding a pinch of baking soda to cooking water helps older beans soften more quickly.

COMPLETE PROTEIN CHILI MIX

This hearty meal combines beans with meat powder and spices for a satisfying, long-storing complete meal.

Ingredients:

- ¼ cup tomato powder (or ½ cup dried tomato flakes)
- 1 cup dried kidney beans
- 1 cup meat powder
- ½ cup dried bell peppers
- ¼ cup dried onion flakes
- 3 tablespoons chili powder
- 1 tablespoon cumin
- 1 tablespoon garlic powder
- 1 teaspoon cayenne pepper (adjust to taste)

- 1 teaspoon black pepper
- 2 teaspoons salt

Instructions:

1. Package in gallon-sized Mylar bags with 500cc oxygen absorbers
2. Seal and label with cooking instructions

To Cook: Soak beans overnight or use quick-soak method. Cook beans in 8 cups water until tender (1-2 hours). Add meat powder and seasonings, simmer 30 minutes. Add water as needed for desired consistency.

PROTEIN STORAGE SUMMARY

Building a diverse protein storage system ensures you have options and nutrition for the long term. Aim for a combination of:

- Dried jerky and meat powder for lightweight, compact storage
- Canned meats for convenience and variety
- Dried beans and legumes for affordable, complete protein
- Powdered milk and eggs for baking and nutrition

In the next chapter, we'll explore the foundation of any food storage system: grains, starches, and vegetables that provide energy, fiber, and essential nutrients.

CHAPTER 4: STAPLES, GRAINS & VEGETABLES

Grains and starches form the foundation of long-term food storage. They're affordable, calorie-dense, store beautifully for decades, and provide the energy your body needs to function. Combined with the proteins from the previous chapter and the vegetables we'll preserve here, you'll have everything needed for complete, satisfying meals.

LONG-TERM GRAIN STORAGE

Not all grains store equally. Whole grains containing natural oils (like brown rice, whole wheat berries, and oats with the germ intact) have shorter shelf lives—typically 1-3 years even when properly stored. For maximum longevity, focus on processed grains with oils removed.

Best Grains for 25+ Year Storage:

- Pasta (all varieties)
- White flour (not whole wheat)
- Rolled oats (not steel-cut)
- Cornmeal (degerminated)

- Pearled barley

Storage Method for Grains:

1. Purchase grains in bulk from restaurant supply stores, co-ops, or online retailers
2. Inspect for moisture, insects, or debris
3. Package in Mylar bags sized appropriately for your use (gallon bags for small families, five-gallon bucket liners for bulk storage)
4. Add oxygen absorbers (300cc for gallon bags, 2000cc for five-gallon buckets)
5. Seal with a heat sealer, removing as much air as possible
6. Place sealed bags in food-grade buckets for protection
7. Label clearly with contents, quantity, and date

Rice Storage Example:

A five-gallon bucket holds approximately 35 pounds of white rice—enough for one person for 3-4 months or a family of four for about one month. For a one-year supply for a family of four, you'll need approximately 12-15 buckets of rice.

PASTA: THE VERSATILE STAPLE

Pasta is a prepper's dream. It stores for 30+ years when properly sealed, cooks quickly, requires minimal fuel, and comes in dozens of shapes and sizes for variety. Stock multiple types to prevent food fatigue.

Recommended Pasta Varieties:

- Penne or rigatoni (holds sauce well)
- Elbow macaroni (for mac and cheese)
- Egg noodles (for soups and casseroles)
- Small shapes like orzo or ditalini (for soups)

PASTA PRIMAVERA MIX

This complete meal kit combines pasta with vegetables and seasonings for a quick, satisfying dinner.

Ingredients:

- 2 cups dried pasta (penne, rotini, or macaroni)
- 1 cup dried mixed vegetables (carrots, peas, corn, green beans)
- ½ cup dried bell peppers
- ¼ cup dried tomato flakes
- 2 tablespoons dried onion flakes
- 2 tablespoons Italian seasoning

- 1 tablespoon garlic powder
- 2 teaspoons salt
- 1 teaspoon black pepper
- ½ cup powdered Parmesan cheese (optional, reduces shelf life slightly)

Instructions:

1. Package dried pasta in one quart-sized bag with an oxygen absorber. Combine vegetables and seasonings in another quart bag with an oxygen absorber.
2. Place both bags in a gallon bag or small container
3. Label with cooking instructions

To Cook: Boil pasta according to package directions. During last 5 minutes of cooking, add vegetable mix. Drain, toss with a little oil or butter if available, and season to taste.

DEHYDRATING AND STORING VEGETABLES

Vegetables provide essential vitamins, minerals, fiber, and flavor to your storage system. While commercially freeze-dried vegetables are excellent, dehydrating your own is much more affordable and works beautifully for long-term storage.

Best Vegetables for Dehydration:

- Celery (slice thin)
- Onions (dice or make flakes)
- Bell peppers (dice)
- Tomatoes (slice or make powder)
- Corn (use frozen corn, spread on trays)
- Peas (use frozen, dehydrate until hard)
- Green beans (cut into 1-inch pieces)
- Mushrooms (slice thin)
- Potatoes (dice or make flakes)

Dehydration Process:

1. Wash and prepare vegetables (peel if desired, dice or slice uniformly)
2. Blanch vegetables briefly in boiling water (1-3 minutes) to preserve color and nutrients
3. Plunge into ice water to stop cooking
4. Drain thoroughly and pat dry
5. Arrange on dehydrator trays in single layer without overlapping
6. Dehydrate at 125-135°F until completely dry and brittle (6-12 hours depending on vegetable)
7. Allow to cool completely

8. Package immediately in Mylar bags with oxygen absorbers
9. Seal and label

Rehydration: Most vegetables rehydrate in hot water in 15-30 minutes. Use approximately 1 cup dried vegetables to 2 cups hot water. For soups and stews, add dried vegetables directly to the pot—they'll rehydrate as the dish cooks.

VEGETABLE SOUP BASE

This versatile mix creates the foundation for countless soups and stews.

Ingredients:

- 1 cup dried celery
- 1 cup dried onions
- 1 cup dried bell peppers
- ½ cup dried tomato flakes
- ½ cup dried corn
- ½ cup dried peas
- ¼ cup dried parsley

Instructions:

1. Divide into portions (about 1 cup per quart bag)
2. Package in Mylar bags with 300cc oxygen absorbers
3. Seal and label

To Use: Add one package to any soup or stew recipe, or combine with bouillon and grains for a simple vegetable soup.

POTATO PRODUCTS

Potatoes are comfort food and a valuable source of calories, potassium, and vitamin C. While fresh potatoes don't store long-term, potato products do.

Potato Flakes (Instant Mashed Potatoes):

Dehydrated Potato Dice:

1. Peel and dice potatoes into ¼-inch cubes
2. Blanch in boiling water for 5 minutes
3. Drain and spread on dehydrator trays
4. Dehydrate at 135°F for 8-12 hours until completely dry and hard
5. Package in Mylar with oxygen absorbers

To Use: Rehydrate in hot water for 20-30 minutes, then use in any potato recipe. Add directly to soups and stews.

LOADED POTATO SOUP MIX

This hearty, comforting soup stores for years and tastes like home.

Ingredients:

- 2 cups instant potato flakes (or 1½ cups dried potato dices)
- 1 cup powdered milk
- ½ cup dried onion flakes
- ¼ cup dried celery
- 3 tablespoons chicken bouillon powder
- 2 tablespoons dried chives
- 1 tablespoon garlic powder
- 1 teaspoon black pepper
- ½ teaspoon dried thyme

Instructions:

1. Package in quart Mylar bags (about 1½ cups per serving for 4 people)
2. Add 300cc oxygen absorbers
3. Seal and label

To Cook: Add one package to 6 cups boiling water, whisk until smooth, reduce heat and simmer 10 minutes. For extra richness, stir in a little butter or oil if available. Top with crumbled bacon or jerky bits if desired.

COMBINING GRAINS AND VEGETABLES

The real magic happens when you combine grains, vegetables, and proteins into complete meal kits. These assemblies make meal planning during emergencies simple and ensure balanced nutrition.

HEARTY RICE AND VEGETABLE PILAF

Ingredients:

- 2 cups long-grain white rice (or parboiled rice for longer shelf life)
- 1 cup dried mixed vegetables
- ¼ cup dried onion flakes
- 2 tablespoons chicken or vegetable bouillon powder
- 1 tablespoon dried parsley
- 1 teaspoon garlic powder
- ½ teaspoon black pepper

Instructions:

1. Mix ingredients in Mylar bag, add 500cc oxygen absorber, seal & label.

To Cook: Add package to 5 cups boiling water, reduce heat, cover and simmer 20-25 minutes until rice is tender and liquid is absorbed.

With your grains, vegetables, and proteins stored, you have the core of a complete food system. In the next chapter, we'll add the elements that make food enjoyable: flavor, comfort, and nutrition boosters that turn survival rations into satisfying meals.

CHAPTER 5: FLAVOR, NUTRITION & COMFORT

Survival food doesn't have to be bland or boring. In fact, maintaining morale during difficult times may depend as much on flavorful, comforting food as on calories and nutrition. This chapter focuses on the herbs, spices, comfort foods, and nutritional supplements that transform basic staples into meals you'll actually look forward to eating.

HERBS AND SPICES

Properly stored herbs and spices last for years and take up minimal space. They're lightweight, inexpensive, and make the difference between eating to survive and eating to thrive.

Essential Spices for Long-Term Storage:

- Black pepper
- Garlic powder
- Onion powder
- Chili powder
- Cumin

- Paprika
- Cinnamon
- Italian seasoning blend
- Dried oregano
- Dried basil
- Dried thyme
- Dried parsley
- Bay leaves
- Red pepper flakes
- Curry powder

DIY SEASONING BLENDS

Creating your own seasoning blends saves money and ensures you have exactly the flavors you want.

Taco Seasoning Mix

Ingredients:

- 1 tablespoon chili powder
- ¼ cup cumin
- ¼ cup paprika
- 3 tablespoons onion powder
- 2 tablespoons garlic powder
- 2 tablespoons dried oregano
- 1 tablespoon black pepper
- 1 tablespoon salt
- 1 teaspoon cayenne pepper (adjust to taste)

Instructions:

1. Package in small Mylar bags or jars
2. Use 2-3 tablespoons per pound of meat or beans

Italian Seasoning Blend

Ingredients:

- 1 tablespoon dried basil
- ¼ cup dried oregano
- ¼ cup dried parsley
- 2 tablespoons dried thyme
- 2 tablespoons dried rosemary (crushed)
- 1 tablespoon garlic powder
- 1 tablespoon onion powder

Instructions:

1. Store in airtight container
2. Use in pasta dishes, soups, and Italian-style meals

BOUILLON AND SOUP BASES

Bouillon cubes, granules, and powders are concentrated flavor bombs that store for years and add depth to any dish. Stock multiple varieties for versatility.

Recommended Bouillon Types:

- Beef bouillon
- Vegetable bouillon
- Ham or pork bouillon

Storage: Keep bouillon in original packaging if unopened, or transfer to Mylar bags with oxygen absorbers after opening. Properly stored bouillon lasts 10+ years.

Uses Beyond Soup:

- Mix into meat powder when rehydrating
- Use as seasoning for vegetables
- Create quick gravies and sauces

BAKING ESSENTIALS

The ability to bake bread, biscuits, and treats during difficult times provides both nutrition and enormous psychological comfort.

Long-Term Baking Supplies:

- Sugar (stores indefinitely)
- Brown sugar (stores indefinitely if kept dry)
- Baking powder (stores 1-2 years; buy in bulk and rotate)
- Baking soda (stores indefinitely)
- Salt
- Powdered milk
- Powdered eggs
- Shortening (stores 3-5 years unopened)
- Honey (stores indefinitely)
- Vanilla extract (stores indefinitely)

BISCUIT MIX

This homemade biscuit mix stores for years and makes quick, comforting bread with minimal effort.

Ingredients:

- 10 cups all-purpose flour
- ½ cup baking powder
- ¼ cup sugar
- 2 tablespoons salt
- 2 cups powdered milk
- 2 cups shortening

Instructions:

1. In a large bowl, combine flour, baking powder, sugar, salt, and powdered milk. Cut in shortening until mixture resembles coarse crumbs.
2. Package in gallon Mylar bags (about 4 cups per bag) with oxygen absorbers
3. Seal and label

To Make Biscuits: Combine 2 cups mix with ½ cup water. Knead briefly, pat out to ½-inch thickness, cut into rounds. Bake at 450°F for 10-12 minutes.

Notes: This mix also works for pancakes (add extra water for thinner batter) and as a coating for fried foods.

COMFORT FOODS AND TREATS

Never underestimate the power of comfort food to lift spirits and maintain morale. Include treats and familiar favorites in your storage system.

Hot Chocolate Mix

Ingredients:

- 4 cups powdered milk (or non-dairy creamer for longer shelf life)
- 2 cups unsweetened cocoa powder
- 2 cups sugar
- 1 teaspoon salt

Instructions:

1. Package in quart Mylar bags with oxygen absorbers
2. Use ⅓ cup mix per cup of hot water

NUTRITIONAL SUPPLEMENTS

While a well-balanced storage system provides good nutrition, supplements offer insurance against deficiencies.

NUTRITIONAL DRINK MIX

This homemade mix provides protein, calories, and nutrients in an easy-to-prepare drink.

Ingredients:

- 2 cups powdered milk or non-dairy creamer (for smoother texture and better nutrition)
- 2 cups protein powder (whey or plant-based)
- 1 cup sugar or powdered honey
- ½ cup unsweetened cocoa powder
- ¼ cup powdered peanut butter (optional)
- 2 tablespoons vanilla powder or extract

Instructions:

1. Package in quart Mylar bags with oxygen absorbers
2. Use ½ cup mix per cup of water

Notes: This provides approximately 200-300 calories and 15-20 grams of protein per serving. Excellent for quick nutrition during high-stress situations.

FLAVOR ROTATION STRATEGY

Even with excellent variety, food fatigue can set in if you eat the same things repeatedly. Combat this by:

- Creating multiple versions of basic meals with different seasonings
- Rotating through different grains (rice one week, pasta the next)
- Varying protein sources (beans, meat powder, canned meats)
- Adding different vegetables to similar base recipes

With flavor, comfort, and nutrition covered, you have nearly everything needed for a complete food system. In the next chapter, we'll address the final essentials: water, fats, and cooking methods.

CHAPTER 6: WATER, FATS & COOKING ESSENTIALS

Food is only half the equation. Without water for drinking, cooking, and rehydrating your stored foods, even the best food storage system is useless. Similarly, fats and oils provide essential nutrition, and having reliable cooking methods ensures you can actually prepare your stored food when needed.

WATER STORAGE

The human body can survive weeks without food, but only days without water. Plan for a minimum of one gallon per person per day—half for drinking, half for cooking and hygiene.

Short-Term Water Storage (1-2 weeks)

Long-Term Water Storage (months to years)

Water Storage Containers:

- 15-gallon barrels (good for small spaces)
- 55-gallon drums (excellent for long-term bulk storage)

- Water bricks or boxes (stackable and space-efficient)

Important: Never store water containers directly on concrete. Use pallets or plastic sheeting to prevent chemical leaching.

WATER PURIFICATION

Stored water can become contaminated, or you may need to purify water from questionable sources. Have multiple purification methods available.

- Boiling
- Water Purification Tablets
- Water Filters
- Bleach

Storage: Keep purification supplies in your storage area along with your food. Rotate tablets and bleach every 2-3 years for maximum effectiveness.

COOKING FATS AND OILS

Fats are essential for health, providing energy, supporting hormone production, and enabling absorption of fat-soluble vitamins. They're also the most challenging food category to store long-term because fats oxidize and go rancid.

- Best Fats for Long-Term Storage
- Coconut Oil
- Ghee (Clarified Butter)
- Shortening
- Olive Oil

HOMEMADE GHEE

Making your own ghee is simple and creates a shelf-stable fat perfect for long-term storage.

Ingredients:

- 2 pounds unsalted butter

Instructions:

1. Melt over medium-low heat without stirring
2. Butter will foam, then become clear with milk solids settling to the bottom
3. Continue cooking until milk solids turn golden brown and butter smells nutty (20-30 minutes)
4. Remove from heat and let cool slightly

5. Strain through cheesecloth or fine mesh strainer into clean, dry jars
6. Seal jars and store in a cool, dark location

Notes: Properly made ghee stores for 1-2 years at room temperature, longer if refrigerated. Two pounds of butter yields approximately 1½ pounds of ghee.

EMERGENCY COOKING METHODS

During power outages or emergencies, you'll need alternative cooking methods to prepare your stored food.

- Camping Stoves
- Rocket Stoves
- Solar Ovens
- Dutch Oven Cooking

Fuel Storage:

- Butane canisters: Store in cool, dry location; rotate every 5 years
- Charcoal: Stores indefinitely if kept dry
- Wood: Free and renewable; requires storage space and drying time

REHYDRATION TECHNIQUES

Most of your stored food will be dehydrated and require rehydration before eating. Understanding proper techniques ensures best results.

Cold Water Rehydration: A gentle method of restoring dried foods by soaking them in cool or room-temperature water for several hours, ideal for preserving texture and nutrients in delicate items like fruits or jerky.

Hot Water Rehydration: A faster process that uses boiling or near-boiling water to quickly soften and revive dried foods, commonly used for soups, stews, and meals that will be served warm.

Cooking Rehydration: A method where dried foods are added directly into a simmering dish, allowing them to absorb liquid and cook simultaneously—perfect for hearty recipes like stews, casseroles, or one-pot meals.

Rehydration Ratios:

- Fruits: 1 cup dried to 1½ cups water
- Beans: 1 cup dried to 3 cups water
- Meat powder: 1 cup powder to 1 cup water

OFF-GRID COOKING TIPS

Conserve Fuel:

- Bring food to a boil, then use retained heat (wrap pot in towels) to finish cooking
- Combine foods that cook in similar times in one pot
- Soak beans and grains before cooking to reduce cooking time

Maximize Efficiency:

- Cook larger batches and reheat portions rather than cooking multiple small meals
- Use pressure cookers when possible—they reduce cooking time by 70%

Safety:

- Keep fire extinguishers accessible
- Store fuel away from heat sources and living areas
- Ensure adequate ventilation for all cooking methods

With water, fats, and cooking methods secured, you have all the components needed for a complete survival food system. In the next chapter, we'll put it all together by creating complete food buckets and emergency kits ready for immediate use.

CHAPTER 7: DIY FOOD BUCKETS & EMERGENCY KITS

Now comes the satisfying part: assembling complete, ready-to-use food buckets and emergency kits. These pre-planned systems eliminate guesswork during stressful times and ensure you have balanced, complete nutrition organized and ready to go.

THE BUCKET SYSTEM

Five-gallon food-grade buckets are the backbone of long-term food storage. They're affordable (often free from bakeries or restaurants), stackable, rodent-proof, and protect contents from light, moisture, and physical damage.

Bucket Organization Strategies: Methods used to categorize and store long-term food supplies in bulk containers for easier access, rotation, and inventory management.

Single-Ingredient Buckets: Buckets filled with one staple item—such as rice, beans, or flour—making it simple to track quantities and restock specific ingredients as needed.

Meal-Kit Buckets: Pre-assembled buckets containing all the dry ingredients for complete meals, allowing for quick, ready-to-cook options during emergencies or busy times.

Themed Buckets: Buckets organized around specific purposes or cuisines—like breakfast foods, soups, or baking supplies—to make meal planning and preparation more efficient.

CREATING COMPLETE MEAL BUCKETS

The most practical approach for emergency preparedness is creating buckets that contain everything needed for multiple complete meals.

30-DAY DINNER BUCKET

This bucket provides dinner for one person for 30 days or a family of four for one week.

Contents:

- 5 pounds dried beans (mixed varieties, in 1-pound bags)
- 3 pounds pasta (various shapes, in 1-pound bags)
- 5 pounds white rice (in 1-pound bags)
- 2 pounds dried vegetables (mixed, in ½-pound bags)
- 1 pound meat powder (in ¼-pound bags)
- 8 ounces bouillon powder (chicken and beef, in separate bags)
- 4 ounces mixed seasonings (Italian, taco, curry blends in separate bags)
- 2 ounces salt and pepper
- 1 pound tomato powder or sauce mix (optional, for stews and pasta dishes)

Assembly Instructions:

1. Ensure each ingredient bag is sealed airtight before placing into the bucket.
2. Line bucket with 5-gallon Mylar bag
3. Arrange sealed ingredient bags in bucket
4. Add 2000cc oxygen absorber to bucket
5. Seal bucket liner
6. Snap on lid
7. Label exterior with contents, date, and meal count

7-DAY BREAKFAST BUCKET

Everything needed for one week of hearty breakfasts for a family of four.

Contents:

- 3 pounds powdered milk
- 2 pounds dried fruit mix
- 3 pounds rolled oats or instant oatmeal (in 1-pound bags)
- 1 pound brown sugar
- 8 ounces cinnamon and spices
- 4 ounces salt
- 2 pounds pancake/biscuit mix
- 1 pound honey powder or sugar
- 8 ounces powdered eggs

Assembly Instructions

- Seal all dry ingredients in sturdy, food-grade bags.
- Line a 5-gallon bucket with a Mylar liner.
- Arrange sealed ingredient bags neatly in the bucket (heavier items like powdered milk and pancake mix at the bottom).
- Add one **2000cc oxygen absorber** inside the liner.
- Press out excess air and heat-seal or zip the Mylar liner securely.
- Snap on the lid tightly to ensure an airtight seal.
- Label the exterior with **"7-Day Breakfast Bucket"**, the **contents list**, and the **date of packaging**.

EMERGENCY 3-DAY KIT

A compact bucket designed for grab-and-go emergency evacuation.

Contents:

- 3 liters bottled water (or pouches if space allows)
- 6 instant oatmeal packets
- 3 pounds dried fruit and nuts
- 2 pounds jerky
- 6 instant rice or pasta meals
- Water purification tablets
- Disposable utensils and bowls
- Can opener
- Matches or lighter
- Cooking instructions

Assembly Instructions:

1. Use a **3- or 4-gallon bucket** for easy portability.
2. Pack food items first—layer **oatmeal packets, dried fruit/nuts, jerky, and instant meals** for even weight distribution.
3. Place **non-food items** (utensils, can opener, purification tablets, matches, cooking instructions) on top in a sealed zip bag to keep them dry.

4. If using Mylar liners for food pouches, include one **1000cc oxygen absorber** before sealing.
5. Close bucket securely with a snap-on or gamma lid.
6. Label clearly: **"3-Day Emergency Food & Supply Kit"** and note the **packing date**.
7. Store in an accessible location near your evacuation route or vehicle.

BUDGET-FRIENDLY BUILDING STRATEGY

Building a complete food storage system can seem overwhelming, but a systematic approach makes it affordable and achievable.

Month 1: Foundation

- 50 pounds rice ($20-30)
- 25 pounds beans ($15-20)
- 10 pounds pasta ($10)
- Salt, sugar, basic spices ($10)
- **Total: $55-70**

Month 2: Proteins

- 20 cans tuna or chicken ($20-30)
- Ingredients for homemade jerky ($30)
- 10 pounds dried beans (additional varieties) ($10)
- **Total: $60-70**

Month 3: Vegetables and Flavor

- Dehydrator ($40-60, one-time investment)
- Fresh vegetables for dehydrating ($20)
- Bouillon, spices, seasonings ($20)
- **Total: $80-100**

Month 4: Baking and Comfort

- 25 pounds flour ($10)
- 10 pounds sugar ($5)
- Powdered milk ($20)
- Coffee, tea, cocoa ($15)
- **Total: $50**

Month 5: Fats and Supplements

- Coconut oil ($15)
- Shortening ($10)
- Multivitamins ($15)

- Honey ($10)
- **Total: $50**

Month 6: Equipment and Containers

- Mylar bags (100-pack) ($25)
- Oxygen absorbers (100-pack) ($20)
- 5-gallon buckets (6 buckets) ($0-30, often free)
- Heat sealer ($30)
- **Total: $75-105**

Six-Month Total: $370-465

This provides a substantial foundation. Continue adding monthly, focusing on expanding quantities and variety.

INVENTORY AND ORGANIZATION

A well-organized system saves time, reduces waste, and provides confidence in your preparedness.

Inventory Spreadsheet:

- Item name and category
- Quantity and unit size
- Storage location
- Packaging date
- Expiration or rotation date
- Notes (source, price, special instructions)

Color-Coding System:

- Red: Proteins
- Yellow: Grains and starches
- Green: Vegetables
- Blue: Baking and sweets
- Orange: Fats and oils
- Purple: Spices and seasonings

Rotation Schedule:

- Mark each container with packaging date
- Store newest items in back, oldest in front
- Plan to use and replace items every 5-10 years
- Conduct annual inventory checks

STORAGE LOCATION PLANNING

Ideal Storage Conditions:

- Humidity: Below 15%
- Light: Complete darkness or opaque containers
- Accessibility: Organized for easy access and rotation

Storage Locations:

- Closets (interior closets maintain stable temperatures)
- Under beds (use flat storage containers)
- Garage (only if temperature-controlled)
- Dedicated pantry or storage room

What to Avoid:

- Damp basements (moisture and flooding risk)
- Near heat sources (furnaces, water heaters)
- Direct sunlight
- Concrete floors without barriers

PACKING LISTS AND DOCUMENTATION

For each bucket or kit, create a detailed packing list including:

- Complete contents with quantities
- Packaging date
- Estimated shelf life
- Cooking instructions for each item
- Calorie and serving information
- Special notes or warnings

Laminate these lists and attach to bucket lids, or store in waterproof bags inside buckets. In an emergency, you'll know exactly what you have and how to use it without opening every container.

With your buckets assembled, organized, and documented, you have a complete, ready-to-use food storage system. In the next chapter, we'll discuss how to actually live with and use your storage—making it a practical part of daily life rather than an untouched emergency reserve.

CHAPTER 8: PRACTICAL LIVING FROM YOUR STORAGE

A food storage system that sits untouched for years isn't truly useful. The best approach is integrating your stored foods into regular meal planning, learning to cook with them, and maintaining a rotation system that keeps everything fresh and familiar. This chapter shows you how to make your storage system a living, practical part of your household.

COOKING WITH STORED FOODS

The first step in making your storage practical is learning to cook with dehydrated and preserved ingredients. These foods behave differently than fresh ingredients, and understanding how to work with them ensures successful, delicious meals.

Rehydration Timing:
Each food type absorbs moisture at a different rate. Grains and beans may need soaking or simmering, while vegetables and meats can often be rehydrated directly in soups or stews. Always allow enough time for ingredients to fully absorb water before seasoning or combining with others.

Flavor Development:
Stored foods often taste better when given time to "marry" in a recipe. Soups, stews, and casseroles made with dehydrated ingredients benefit from slow cooking,

allowing flavors to deepen and balance. A small amount of fat or acid (like butter, oil, or vinegar) can help restore brightness and richness to long-stored foods.

Texture Considerations:
Dehydrated and preserved foods may not return to their exact original texture. Vegetables may be softer, and meats slightly chewier. Use these traits to your advantage—softer ingredients are perfect for soups and sauces, while firmer ones add body to casseroles or skillet meals.

WEEKLY MEAL PLAN USING STORAGE FOODS

Monday: Vegetable Soup

Use your vegetable soup base mix, add bouillon, and simmer with pasta or rice. Serve with homemade biscuits from your baking mix.

Tuesday: Chili

Prepare your complete protein chili mix. Serve over rice or with cornbread made from stored cornmeal.

Wednesday: Pasta Primavera

Cook your pasta primavera meal kit. Add canned chicken or tuna for extra protein.

Thursday: Rice and Beans

Prepare your rice and beans meal kit. Top with dried salsa or hot sauce from storage.

Friday: Loaded Potato Soup

Make your potato soup mix. Serve with jerky pieces or crumbled bacon if available.

Saturday: Breakfast for Dinner

Pancakes from your biscuit mix, served with rehydrated fruit and honey.

Sunday: Hearty Stew

Combine meat powder, dried vegetables, potato dice, and bouillon for a comforting stew. Serve with biscuits.

ROTATION SYSTEM IN PRACTICE

Effective rotation ensures you're always using the oldest items first while maintaining a full storage system.

First In, First Out (FIFO):

Rotation Schedule:

- **Quarterly:** Conduct inventory check, note items approaching rotation dates
- **Annually:** Deep inventory, plan major rotation and replacement
- **Every 5 years:** Major rotation cycle, use and replace significant quantities

Rotation Cooking Days:

TESTING AND ADJUSTING

Your storage system should evolve based on your family's preferences and experiences. What looks good on paper may need fine-tuning once you start cooking from your supply. Regular testing ensures that the food you store is food your family actually enjoys and uses.

Taste Testing: Periodically sample items from your long-term storage to ensure quality and flavor haven't diminished. This not only helps rotate your stock but also familiarizes your family with the taste and texture of preserved foods before they're needed in an emergency.

Cooking Tests: Practice preparing complete meals using only stored ingredients. This helps you adjust rehydration times, seasoning levels, and cooking methods. Keep notes on what works best, and update your recipes accordingly for smoother future meal prep.

Family Feedback: Involve everyone in evaluating meals made from your storage foods. If a dish is too salty, bland, or unappealing, adjust seasoning blends or ingredient ratios. Over time, this feedback will help you build a storage system tailored to your family's actual tastes and needs.

MAINTAINING FRESHNESS

Even with proper storage, periodic checks ensure your system remains in good condition.

Inspection Checklist:

- Inspect buckets for damage, pest activity, or moisture

- Verify oxygen absorbers were activated (they should be hard and solid)
- Look for any signs of spoilage, off odors, or discoloration
- Test a small sample if you have any concerns

When to Discard:

- Packages with broken seals or compromised containers
- Foods stored in improper conditions (heat, moisture, light)
- Anything that doesn't look, smell, or taste right

RESTOCKING AND EXPANSION

As you use items from storage, replace them promptly to maintain your supply level.

Restocking Strategy:

- Buy in bulk when prices are favorable
- Take advantage of sales and seasonal pricing
- Gradually increase quantities as budget allows

Expansion Priorities:

1. Increase quantities of favorites
2. Add variety within existing categories
3. Include special dietary needs or preferences
4. Build redundancy in critical items
5. Add comfort foods and treats

TEACHING OTHERS

Your food storage knowledge is valuable. Share it with family members so everyone can use the system effectively.

Family Training:

- Teach basic cooking skills with stored ingredients
- Practice emergency meal preparation together
- Explain labeling and inventory systems
- Ensure multiple people can operate sealing equipment

Documentation:

- Storage location map
- Inventory overview
- Basic recipes and cooking instructions
- Equipment operation guides

- Rotation schedule and procedures

LIVING THE SELF-RELIANT LIFESTYLE

Integrating food storage into daily life creates genuine self-reliance rather than just emergency preparedness.

Benefits of Regular Use:

- Familiarity with flavors and textures
- Practiced efficiency in meal preparation
- Natural rotation without waste
- Peace of mind from proven systems

Mindset Shift:

With your storage system integrated into daily life, you've achieved true food security. In the final chapter, we'll explore the deeper meaning of self-reliance and the peace of mind that comes from genuine preparedness.

CHAPTER 9: MINDSET OF THE SELF-RELIANT SURVIVOR

Building a 25-year food supply is a practical accomplishment, but it's also something deeper—a statement of independence, a commitment to self-reliance, and a return to the wisdom our ancestors understood instinctively. This final chapter explores the mindset that makes preparedness not just effective, but empowering and sustainable.

THE PEACE OF TRUE PREPAREDNESS

There's a unique sense of calm that comes from knowing you're prepared. When news reports discuss supply chain disruptions, economic uncertainty, or natural disasters, you can listen without panic. You've taken practical steps to protect your family, and that knowledge provides genuine peace of mind.

This isn't about fear or paranoia. It's about responsibility and wisdom. Just as you maintain insurance, emergency funds, and first aid supplies, food storage is simply prudent planning. The difference is that food storage is something you can build yourself, control completely, and use regardless of circumstances.

The Confidence of Capability:

LEARNING FROM OUR ANCESTORS

For most of human history, food preservation wasn't a hobby or fringe activity—it was essential for survival. Every culture developed methods to store food through lean times: drying, smoking, salting, fermenting, and storing grains and roots.

Our great-grandparents would find our modern dependence on grocery stores and just-in-time supply chains baffling and risky. They understood that self-reliance meant having food put by, skills to preserve more, and the knowledge to make do with what they had.

Traditional Wisdom:

- "A full pantry is a full heart"
- "The best time to prepare for winter is summer"
- "Waste not, want not"

These aren't just quaint sayings—they're practical philosophy born from experience. By building your food storage system, you're reconnecting with this wisdom and applying it to modern circumstances.

BUILDING INDEPENDENCE, NOT FEAR

The preparedness community sometimes gets painted with a broad brush of extremism or paranoia. But true preparedness isn't about fear—it's about independence and responsibility.

What Preparedness Is:

- Building skills and knowledge
- Creating resilience against uncertainty
- Achieving independence from fragile systems
- Connecting with traditional wisdom and practices

What Preparedness Isn't:

- Isolating from community
- Hoarding at others' expense
- Obsessing over worst-case scenarios
- Neglecting present life for future concerns

The goal is balance—being prepared enough to handle disruptions while still living fully in the present. Your food storage should provide security, not consume your life with worry.

THE RIPPLE EFFECT OF SELF-RELIANCE

When you become more self-reliant, the benefits extend far beyond your immediate household. Every jar you fill, every garden you tend, and every skill you learn contributes to something larger—creating stability, confidence, and community resilience that others can feel and follow.

Community Strength:
When families take responsibility for their own food and resources, the entire community grows stronger. Neighbors who preserve, share, and trade can weather hard times together, reducing dependence on fragile supply chains and outside systems.

Teaching and Sharing:
Passing on these skills—whether to your children, friends, or neighbors—keeps old traditions alive. Teaching someone how to can, cure, or dehydrate food not only preserves knowledge but also fosters a sense of purpose and connection between generations.

Economic Independence:
Self-reliance naturally leads to financial freedom. Growing, preserving, and preparing your own food reduces grocery costs, limits waste, and provides peace of mind knowing that your family's well-being doesn't hinge on fluctuating markets or shortages.

MAINTAINING THE MINDSET

Preparedness is a journey, not a destination. Maintaining the right mindset ensures long-term success and satisfaction. Over time, your skills, systems, and understanding will grow—but so will your appreciation for the simple peace that comes from being ready.

Avoid Perfectionism:
It's easy to get caught up in doing everything "just right," but perfection isn't the goal—progress is. Even small steps, like learning a new preservation method or filling one more jar, move you closer to true security.

Stay Flexible:
Life changes, and so will your needs. Be willing to adjust your storage plans, recipes, and methods as your family, climate, or circumstances evolve. Flexibility keeps your preparedness relevant and effective.

Celebrate Progress:
Take pride in what you've accomplished. Every stocked shelf and labeled bucket represents dedication and foresight. Mark milestones—your first full pantry, your first cured ham—and let them remind you of how far you've come.

Share the Journey:
Self-reliance doesn't mean isolation. Encourage others, exchange ideas, and share your successes and lessons learned. Building a community of like-minded people strengthens everyone's preparedness and keeps these traditions alive for future generations.

THE BIGGER PICTURE

Food storage is one component of a resilient, self-reliant lifestyle. As you build confidence in this area, consider expanding to related skills:

Complementary Skills:

- Water collection and purification
- Basic first aid and medical knowledge
- Fire starting and alternative cooking
- Food preservation beyond dehydration (canning, fermenting)
- Basic repairs and maintenance
- Financial preparedness and emergency funds

Each skill adds another layer of resilience and independence.

LIVING WITH PURPOSE

Ultimately, preparedness is about living intentionally rather than reactively. It's choosing to take control of what you can control and accepting what you cannot. It's recognizing that uncertainty is part of life and responding with practical action rather than worry.

Your food storage system represents more than calories and nutrition. It represents your commitment to protecting what matters, your willingness to learn and grow, and your connection to generations of humans who understood that security comes from preparation, not luck.

The True Goal: The goal isn't to hoard or to fear what's ahead—it's to build a steady, peaceful confidence in your ability to provide, no matter the circumstance. Preparedness allows you to live with purpose, generosity, and calm in a world that often feels uncertain. It's about freedom—the kind that comes when you know your family is safe, your shelves are full, and your hands are capable.

MOVING FORWARD

You now have the knowledge to create a complete, long-lasting food storage system. You understand the science of preservation, the techniques for packaging and storing, and the practical skills for using what you've stored. More importantly, you understand the mindset that makes preparedness sustainable and empowering.

Your Next Steps:

1. Test your recipes and adjust based on results
2. Build systematically, adding to your storage each month
3. Practice cooking with stored foods regularly
4. Share your knowledge with others who want to learn
5. Maintain your system with regular checks and rotation
6. Live confidently, knowing you're prepared

The journey to self-reliance is ongoing, but every step forward is valuable. You're not just storing food—you're building security, developing skills, and creating peace of mind for yourself and your family.

Welcome to the community of self-reliant individuals who understand that true security comes not from hoping for the best, but from preparing for whatever comes while living fully in the present. Your shelf-stable survival system is ready. Now go live with confidence, knowing you've taken control of one of life's most fundamental needs.

CONCLUSION

Building a 25-year food storage system is one of the most practical and empowering projects you can undertake. Throughout this book, you've learned the science of food preservation, the techniques for packaging and storing, and the skills for creating complete, nutritious meals that last decades.

You now understand that shelf stability isn't complicated—it's simply controlling moisture, oxygen, light, and temperature. You know how to preserve proteins through drying and dehydration, how to store grains and vegetables for maximum longevity, and how to add the flavors and comfort foods that make meals satisfying rather than just survivable.

You've learned to think in systems rather than individual ingredients, creating complete meal kits and organized buckets that provide balanced nutrition and eliminate guesswork during stressful times. You understand how to calculate your needs, build on a budget, and maintain your system through rotation and regular use.

Most importantly, you've embraced the mindset of self-reliance—the understanding that true security comes from knowledge, preparation, and practical action rather than hope or luck.

Your food storage journey doesn't end with this book. It's an ongoing process of learning, testing, adjusting, and expanding. Start with one bucket, one meal kit, one skill. Build systematically, celebrate your progress, and share your knowledge with others.

The peace of mind that comes from a well-stocked pantry is real and valuable. When uncertainty arises—and it will—you'll face it with confidence, knowing you've taken practical steps to protect what matters most.

You're not just storing food. You're building independence, developing skills, and connecting with the timeless wisdom of self-reliance. That's something worth doing, regardless of what the future holds.

Now go build your shelf-stable survival system. Your future self will thank you.

APPENDIX: THE BIG TABLE OF SHELF STABLE RECIPES!

Recipe Name	Preservation Method	Primary Ingredients	Water to Add / Ratio	Instructions	Shelf Life	Servings / Yield
Cheesy Broccoli Rice Mix	Dry Mix (Mylar + Oxygen Absorber)	1 cup white rice, ¼ cup dried broccoli, 2 tbsp cheese powder, 1 tbsp dried onion flakes, 1 tsp bouillon powder	1 cup mix + 2 cups water	Bring water to a boil, add mix, and simmer 15 minutes until rice is tender. Remove from heat, cover, and rest 5 minutes.	20 years	4 servings
Southwest Lentil Stew	Dehydrated Mix	1 cup lentils, 2 tbsp dried corn, 1 tbsp tomato powder, 1 tsp chili powder, ½ tsp cumin, ¼ tsp garlic powder	1 cup mix + 4 cups water	Combine mix and water in a pot. Simmer 45 minutes until lentils are soft and broth thickens. Salt to taste.	25 years	4 servings
Creamy Mushroom Pasta	Dry Mix (Mylar)	1 cup pasta, ¼ cup dried mushrooms, 2 tbsp milk powder, 1 tbsp onion flakes, ½ tsp garlic powder	1 cup mix + 2 cups water	Boil mix 10–12 minutes until pasta is tender and sauce thickens. Stir often to prevent sticking.	15 years	3 servings
Herbed Couscous Pilaf	Dry Mix (Jar or Mylar)	1 cup couscous, 2 tbsp dried peas, 2 tbsp dried carrots, 1 tsp parsley, ½ tsp salt	1 cup mix + 1 cup boiling water	Pour boiling water over mix, cover 5 minutes, then fluff with fork before serving.	20 years	2 servings
Thai-Style Peanut Noodles	Dry Mix (Mylar or Jar)	1 cup rice noodles, 2 tbsp powdered peanut butter, 1 tbsp soy powder, ¼ tsp chili flakes	1 cup mix + 1 cup hot water	Add hot water, cover 5 minutes, then stir well until sauce coats noodles evenly.	10 years	2 servings
Moroccan Chickpea Tagine	Dehydrated Mix	1 cup dried chickpeas, 2 tbsp dried apricots, 2 tbsp tomato flakes, 1 tsp cinnamon, 1 tsp cumin, ½ tsp garlic powder	1 cup mix + 3 cups water	Soak chickpeas overnight or quick-soak 1 hour. Drain and simmer with water 1 hour until tender.	25 years	4 servings
Vegetable Fried Rice Kit	Dry Mix (Mylar)	1 cup instant rice, ¼ cup dried mixed vegetables, 1 tbsp	1 cup mix + 2	Rehydrate mix 10 minutes in hot water. Drain and	15 years	3 servings

Recipe Name	Preservation Method	Primary Ingredients	Water to Add / Ratio	Instructions	Shelf Life	Servings / Yield
		soy powder, 1 tbsp egg powder, ½ tsp salt	cups water	fry in skillet with oil if available.		
Hearty Split-Pea Curry	Dehydrated Mix	1 cup split peas, ¼ cup dried carrots, 2 tbsp onion flakes, 1 tbsp curry powder, 2 tbsp coconut milk powder	1 cup mix + 4 cups water	Simmer 45 minutes until peas are soft and soup thickens. Stir occasionally.	20 years	4 servings
Tex-Mex Macaroni Skillet	Dry Mix (Mylar)	1 cup elbow macaroni, 2 tbsp tomato powder, 2 tbsp bell pepper, 1 tbsp taco seasoning, 2 tbsp beef TVP	1 cup mix + 3 cups water	Boil 8–10 minutes until pasta is tender and sauce thickens.	20 years	3 servings
Beef-Flavored Ramen Jar	Vacuum-Sealed Jar	1 ramen brick, 1 tsp beef bouillon, 1 tbsp dried cabbage, 1 tbsp onion flakes	2 cups boiling water	Add boiling water, cover, and steep 5 minutes. Stir and serve.	10 years	1 serving
Country Corn Chowder	Dry Mix (Mylar)	1 cup potato flakes, ½ cup dried corn, ¼ cup milk powder, 1 tsp parsley, 1 tbsp bouillon powder	1 cup mix + 6 cups water	Bring water to boil, whisk in mix, and simmer 10 minutes until creamy.	20 years	4 servings
Italian Barley Soup	Dehydrated Mix	1 cup pearled barley, 2 tbsp tomato powder, 2 tbsp onion flakes, 1 tsp basil, 2 tbsp carrot flakes	1 cup mix + 6 cups water	Simmer 1 hour until barley is tender and broth thickens.	25 years	4 servings
Savory Quinoa & Veg Blend	Dehydrated Mix	1 cup quinoa, 2 tbsp peas, 1 tbsp onion flakes, 1 tsp garlic powder, 1 tsp bouillon	1 cup mix + 2 cups water	Simmer 15 minutes, cover, and rest 5 minutes before serving.	20 years	3 servings
Loaded Pasta Alfredo	Dry Mix (Mylar)	1 cup fettuccine, 2 tbsp milk powder, 2 tbsp cheese	1 cup mix + 2	Boil pasta 10 minutes, stirring	15 years	3 servings

Recipe Name	Preservation Method	Primary Ingredients	Water to Add / Ratio	Instructions	Shelf Life	Servings / Yield
		powder, ½ tsp garlic powder	cups water	until sauce thickens and coats noodles.		
Cajun Red Bean Rice	Dehydrated Mix	1 cup red beans, 1 cup rice, 2 tbsp bell pepper, 1 tbsp Cajun seasoning	1 cup mix + 3 cups water	Soak beans overnight, drain, and simmer with mix 1 hour until beans and rice are tender.	25 years	4 servings
Mediterranean Bulgur Bowl	Dry Mix (Mylar)	1 cup bulgur, 2 tbsp tomato flakes, 1 tbsp dried olives, 1 tsp oregano, ½ tsp garlic	1 cup mix + 2 cups boiling water	Add boiling water, cover 15 minutes, and fluff before serving.	15 years	3 servings
Homestyle Chicken Pot Pie Filling	Dry Mix (Mylar)	¼ cup chicken powder, ½ cup dried vegetables, ¼ cup milk powder, 2 tbsp gravy mix	3 cups water	Simmer 10 minutes until thickened. Serve with biscuit mix topping.	20 years	4 servings
Apple Cinnamon Oatmeal	Dry Mix (Mylar)	1 cup oats, 2 tbsp dried apples, 1 tbsp sugar, ½ tsp cinnamon	½ cup mix + 1 cup water	Simmer 3 minutes, stirring, until thick.	25 years	2 servings
Breakfast Hash Mix	Dehydrated Mix	1 cup dried potatoes, 2 tbsp onion flakes, 2 tbsp bell pepper, 2 tbsp bacon-flavored TVP	1 cup mix + 2 cups water	Rehydrate 10 minutes, then pan-fry in oil if available.	10 years	3 servings
Maple Brown Sugar Cream-of-Oats	Dry Mix (Mylar)	1 cup oats, 2 tbsp milk powder, 2 tbsp brown sugar, 1 tsp maple powder	½ cup mix + 1 cup water	Add boiling water, stir well, and serve hot.	20 years	2 servings
Lemon-Herb Orzo	Dry Mix (Mylar)	1 cup orzo, 1 tsp lemon zest, 1 tsp parsley, ½ tsp garlic powder, ½ tsp salt	1 cup mix + 2 cups water	Boil 10 minutes, drain excess liquid, and fluff.	20 years	3 servings

Recipe Name	Preservation Method	Primary Ingredients	Water to Add / Ratio	Instructions	Shelf Life	Servings / Yield
Instant Biscuit Gravy Mix	Dry Mix (Mylar)	¼ cup flour, 2 tbsp milk powder, 2 tbsp sausage TVP, ½ tsp pepper	1½ cups water	Whisk into boiling water and simmer until thickened.	20 years	4 servings
Tropical Rice Pudding	Dry Mix (Mylar)	1 cup rice, 2 tbsp coconut milk powder, 2 tbsp sugar, 2 tbsp dried pineapple	½ cup mix + 1 cup water	Simmer 10 minutes, stirring, until creamy.	15 years	2 servings
Cinnamon Pancake Mix	Dry Mix (Mylar)	1 cup flour, 2 tbsp milk powder, 1 tbsp sugar, 1 tsp baking powder, ½ tsp cinnamon	1 cup mix + ¾ cup water	Mix until smooth and cook on griddle until golden.	10 years	4 servings
Honey Wheat Muffin Mix	Dry Mix (Mylar)	1 cup whole-wheat flour, 2 tbsp honey powder, 2 tbsp milk powder, 1 tsp baking powder	Add water until batter forms	Pour into muffin tins and bake or steam until firm.	10 years	4 muffins
Instant Tomato Basil Soup	Dehydrated Mix	½ cup tomato powder, 2 tbsp milk powder, 1 tsp basil, ½ tsp garlic powder	½ cup mix + 2 cups water	Whisk over medium heat 5 minutes until smooth.	25 years	2 servings
Cheesy Grits	Dry Mix (Mylar)	1 cup grits, 2 tbsp cheese powder, 2 tbsp milk powder, ½ tsp salt	1 cup mix + 3 cups water	Simmer 10 minutes, stirring occasionally.	15 years	3 servings
Asian Rice Porridge	Dry Mix (Mylar)	½ cup rice flakes, 1 tbsp dried onion, ½ tsp ginger powder, 1 tsp soy powder	½ cup mix + 2 cups water	Simmer 15 minutes until thick.	20 years	2 servings
Beefy Noodle Stroganoff	Dry Mix (Mylar)	1 cup egg noodles, 2 tbsp beef TVP, 2 tbsp milk powder, 1 tbsp onion flakes	1 cup mix + 3 cups water	Boil 10 minutes, stirring until creamy and thick.	20 years	3 servings
Creamy Corn Polenta	Dry Mix (Mylar)	½ cup cornmeal, 2 tbsp milk powder,	½ cup mix + 2	Simmer 10 minutes until thick and smooth.	25 years	3 servings

Recipe Name	Preservation Method	Primary Ingredients	Water to Add / Ratio	Instructions	Shelf Life	Servings / Yield
		1 tbsp butter powder, ½ tsp salt	cups water			
Garlic Potato Bisque	Dehydrated Mix	½ cup potato flakes, ½ tsp garlic powder, 2 tbsp milk powder, ½ tsp parsley	½ cup mix + 2 cups hot water	Whisk until smooth and creamy.	20 years	2 servings
Mediterranean Lentil Salad Jar	Dehydrated Mix	1 cup lentils, 1 tbsp tomato flakes, 1 tsp parsley, ½ tsp lemon powder	1 cup mix + 2 cups boiling water	Rehydrate 1 hour, drain, and toss with oil if available.	20 years	3 servings
Taco Rice Jar Meal	Dry Mix (Mylar)	1 cup rice, ½ cup beans, 1 tbsp taco seasoning, 1 tbsp onion flakes	1 cup mix + 2 cups water	Simmer 25 minutes until liquid is absorbed.	25 years	3 servings
Shepherd's Pie Filling	Dehydrated Mix	½ cup potato flakes, ¼ cup beef powder, ¼ cup mixed vegetables, 2 tbsp gravy mix	3 cups water	Simmer 15 minutes until thick.	20 years	4 servings
Creamy Spinach Soup	Dehydrated Mix	¼ cup dried spinach, 2 tbsp milk powder, 1 tbsp onion flakes, pinch nutmeg	1 cup mix + 3 cups water	Blend or whisk over heat until smooth and creamy.	15 years	3 servings
Pumpkin Spice Dessert Mix	Dry Mix (Mylar)	¼ cup pumpkin powder, 2 tbsp sugar, ½ tsp cinnamon, 2 tbsp milk powder	½ cup mix + 1 cup water	Stir and heat until thick and smooth.	10 years	2 servings
Instant Chili Mac	Dry Mix (Mylar)	1 cup macaroni, 2 tbsp tomato powder, 1 tbsp chili powder, 2 tbsp beans, 2 tbsp beef TVP	1 cup mix + 3 cups water	Boil 10 minutes until pasta and beans are tender.	20 years	4 servings
Carrot Ginger Soup	Dehydrated Mix	¼ cup carrot powder, 1 tbsp onion flakes, ½ tsp	1 cup mix + 3 cups water	Simmer 10 minutes, blend until smooth.	15 years	3 servings